MVP SUPERSTARS 2017

Eric Zweig

www.scholastic.ca

Library and Archives Canada Cataloguing in Publication

Zweig, Eric, 1963-, author
MVP superstars 2017 / Eric Zweig.

ISBN 978-1-4431-5769-8 (paperback)

1. Athletes--Biography--Juvenile literature.
2. Athletes--Canada--Biography--Juvenile literature.
I. Title.

GV697.A1Z84 2017   j796.092'2   C2016-906262-7

Photos ©: cover background and throughout: Beholdereye/Dreamstime; cover top left: Allstar Picture Library/ Alamy Images; cover top right: John Russell/Getty Images; cover bottom left: Cal Sport Media/Alamy Images; cover bottom center: Reuters/Alamy Images; cover bottom right: epa european pressphoto agency b.v./Alamy Images; back cover top left: funnybank/iStockphoto; back cover top right: Annsunnyday/Dreamstime; back cover bottom left: Neonnyc/Dreamstime; back cover bottom center: Andrei Krauchuk/Dreamstime; back cover bottom right: obalt88/Dreamstime; 2 background and throughout: Galina Pankratova/Dreamstime; 2 banner and throughout: Hlubokidzianis/Dreamstime; 2 main: Gary A. Vasquez/USA Today; 3 top and throughout: eriksvoboda/iStockphoto; 3 bottom and throughout: funnybank/iStockphoto; 4: Gary A. Vasquez/USA Today; 6: Marc DesRosiers/USA Today; 8: Christopher Hanewinckel/USA Today; 10: PA Images/Alamy Images; 12: Nick Turchiaro/USA Today; 13 and throughout: Andrei Krauchuk/Dreamstime; 14: Geoff Burke/USA Today; 16: John E. Sokolowski/USA Today; 18: Gary A. Vasquez/USA Today; 20: Brad Mills/USA Today; 22: Kelvin Kuo/USA Today; 23 and throughout: Annsunnyday/Dreamstime; 24: Kyle Terada/USA Today; 26: David Richard/USA Today; 28: Kyle Terada/USA Today; 30: Kim Klement/USA Today; 32: J. Carey Lauder/USA Today; 33 and throughout: Neonnyc/Dreamstime; 34: Jeremy Brevard/USA Today; 36: Timothy T. Ludwig/USA Today; 38: Reuters/Alamy Images; 40: Dale Zanine/USA Today; 42: Tom Szczerbowski/USA Today; 43 and throughout: Cobalt88/Dreamstime; 44: Kyle Terada/USA Today; 46: Scott Rovak/USA Today; 48: PA Images/Alamy Images; 50: Matt Kryger/USA Today; 52 left: Bruce Fedyck/USA Today; 52 right: Sergei Belski/USA Today; 53 left: Matt Kartozian/USA Today; 53 right: Kim Klement/USA Today; 54 left: Bob DeChiara/USA Today; 54 right: Brian Spurlock/USA Today; 55 left: Icon Sports Wire/Getty Images; 55 right: Greg M. Cooper/USA Today; 56 left: Kim Klement/USA Today; 56 right: Anne-Marie Sorvin/USA Today.

6 5 4 3 2 1   Printed in Canada 118   17 18 19 20 21

Scholastic Canada Ltd.

Toronto New York London Auckland Sydney
Mexico City New Delhi Hong Kong Buenos Aires

SIDNEY CROSBY

PITTSBURGH PENGUINS

Centre
Height: 1.80 m (5'11")
Weight: 91 kg (200 lbs.)
Born: August 7, 1987, in
Cole Harbour, Nova Scotia

Sidney Crosby was already famous in his hometown of Cole Harbour, Nova Scotia, by the time he was 10 years old. He had plenty of natural talent, but he also had put in the hard work needed to become a star. Crosby was seriously thinking about playing professional hockey by the time he was 14. He was playing hockey on a team with boys three years older than he was. Crosby was still his team's best player, as well as the top scorer in the league, and he led his team to a silver medal at the Canadian midget championship.

Before long Crosby had caught the eye of hockey legend Wayne Gretzky, who predicted that Crosby was the player who might one day break his scoring records. Gretzky was being modest — most of his records still stand — but he could tell that Crosby would be a superstar. Crosby was honoured by the compliment, saying, "I realize there will not be another Gretzky, and I will be the first one to say I will not break his records . . . But for him to say that I could, it means I am doing something right. It was probably the best compliment I could get. I'm going to remember it."

In 2005–2006, when he entered the NHL at age 18 as the number-one draft pick, Crosby became the youngest player ever to score 100 points in a season. A year later, he became the youngest player to lead the NHL in scoring. He also won the Hart Trophy as NHL MVP. In 2009, he became the youngest player to captain a team — the Pittsburgh Penguins — to a Stanley Cup title. Then he led Team Canada to a gold medal at the 2010 Winter Olympics in Vancouver, scoring the winning goal in overtime.

Crosby has never taken his skill for granted and has always worked hard to make himself better. Some of his hardest work was getting back on the ice after a concussion kept him out of action for most of the 2010–2011 and 2011–2012 seasons. There were serious concerns he might never play again, but Crosby came back to play nearly a full season in 2012–2013. Then in 2013–2014, he led the NHL in scoring and was again named MVP. After a slow start in 2015–2016, Crosby had another great season and led the Penguins to a Stanley Cup victory for the second time.

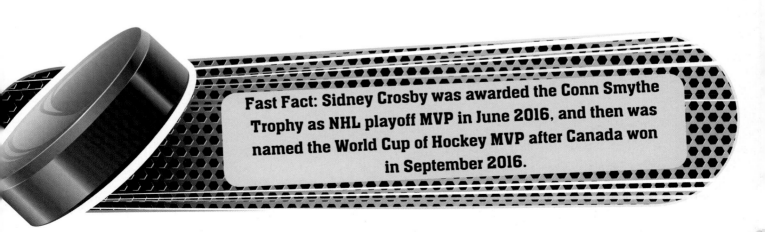

Fast Fact: Sidney Crosby was awarded the Conn Smythe Trophy as NHL playoff MVP in June 2016, and then was named the World Cup of Hockey MVP after Canada won in September 2016.

ALEX OVECHKIN

WASHINGTON CAPITALS

Left Wing
Height: 1.90 m (6'3")
Weight: 108.5 kg (239 lbs.)
Born: September 17, 1985,
in Moscow, USSR
(now Russia)

Alex Ovechkin is one of the greatest scorers in hockey history. He's big and strong, and he can muscle past opponents who try to slow him down.

Athletic talent obviously runs in the family. Ovechkin's father is a former professional soccer player, and his mother won gold medals in basketball for Russia at the 1976 Montreal Olympics and the 1980 Moscow Olympics. Ovechkin's parents knew he would also be an athlete early on — instead of taking the elevator up to his family's 10th-floor apartment, he would run up the stairs.

When he was just two years old, Ovechkin found a hockey stick in a toy store and refused to let go. Whenever he saw a hockey game on television, he would drop all his toys and run to the TV, complaining if his parents tried to change the channel. Still, Ovechkin didn't put on his first pair of skates until he was seven years old. Soon after, he was finally playing hockey at the Moscow Dynamo sports club, but he had to drop out because his parents were so busy with their own athletic careers. A hockey coach at the Dynamo school convinced them to let Ovechkin come back, and by the time he was 16, he was playing for the Moscow Dynamo in Russia's top hockey league, against men who were twice his age.

The Washington Capitals chose Ovechkin first overall in the 2004 NHL Entry Draft, and he joined the team for the 2005–2006 season. That year Ovechkin became just the second player in NHL history to top 50 goals and 100 points in his first season, and he beat out Sidney Crosby as the Rookie of the Year. Two years later Ovechkin led the NHL in goals for the first time, and set a record for the most goals ever scored by a left winger, with 65 on the season.

During the time that Ovechkin has played in the NHL, no other player has come close to scoring as many goals as he has. On January 10, 2016, he scored his 500th career goal. Ovechkin was just the 43rd player in NHL history to reach that milestone, and he's the fifth-fastest ever to accomplish the feat.

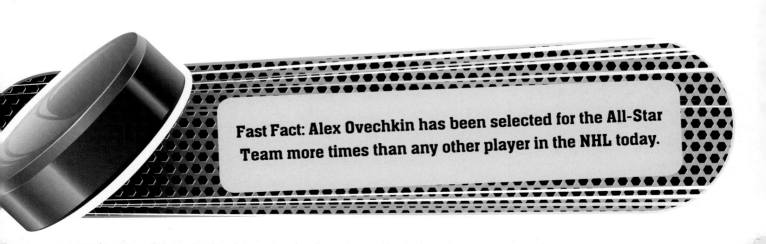

Fast Fact: Alex Ovechkin has been selected for the All-Star Team more times than any other player in the NHL today.

ERIK KARLSSON

OTTAWA SENATORS

Defence
Height: 1.83 m (6'0")
Weight: 87 kg (191 lbs.)
Born: May 31, 1990, in Landsbro, Sweden

Erik Karlsson has explosive speed. He uses his quickness to break up other teams' plays in his end of the ice, as well as to help his own team score goals. These days Karlsson is a star defenceman in the NHL, but when he was 10 years old he wanted to be a goalie. His dad didn't like that idea. "I remember one practice, he came in from the blueline and hit a slapshot right into my chest. I thought I would pass out. I didn't want to be in goal anymore. It might not be the best parenting, but it worked."

Karlsson grew up in Landsbro, a community in the south of Sweden with a population just over 1,400. "There isn't much in the village. A grocery store and a pizzeria . . . Otherwise, there's not much else but an ice rink," Karlsson once told a reporter. "There weren't a lot of people fighting for ice time." When he was 17 years old, Karlsson moved 225 kilometres (140 miles) away from home, to the much larger city of Gothenburg, Sweden. There he joined the Frölunda Hockey Club and helped their junior team win the 2007–2008 national championship. Near the end of that season, he also made his debut with Frölunda's main team — in the top Swedish hockey league. In his very first game, he scored the winning overtime goal on a slapshot to clinch a spot in the playoffs. A few months later, the Ottawa Senators made Karlsson their first pick, 15th overall, in the 2008 NHL Entry Draft. He spent one more year with Frölunda before beginning his NHL career in 2009–2010.

With his blazing speed, pinpoint passes and powerful shot, Karlsson quickly became a star in Ottawa. In his third season, 2011–2012, he won the Norris Trophy as the NHL's best defenceman. At 22 years old, Karlsson was the youngest Norris Trophy winner since 1968, when the legendary Bobby Orr earned his first of a record eight Norris Trophies at the age of 20. Karlsson's play for Sweden earned him the title of Best Defenceman at the 2014 Olympics. He was named captain of the Senators in 2014–2015; that same season he won the Norris Trophy for the second time — and he's a threat to win it again.

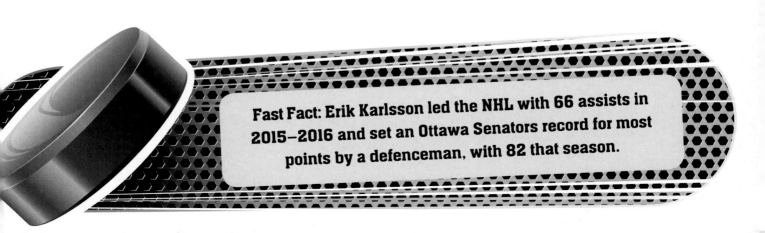

Fast Fact: Erik Karlsson led the NHL with 66 assists in 2015–2016 and set an Ottawa Senators record for most points by a defenceman, with 82 that season.

P.K.
SUBBAN

NASHVILLE PREDATORS

Defence
Height: 1.83 m (6'0")
Weight: 95.5 kg (210 lbs.)
Born: May 13, 1989, in Toronto, Ontario

Fans of the Montreal Canadiens were shocked and saddened when P.K. Subban was traded to the Nashville Predators during the summer of 2016. The team got star player Shea Weber in return, but Subban was a fan favourite during the six seasons he spent with the Habs. He's faced a bit of criticism for his high-risk, big-rewards style of play, but Subban is always exciting to watch! And he's known for his awesome moves off the ice too. He won the hearts of Montrealers when he donated $10 million to the Montreal Children's Hospital in the fall of 2015.

Subban's parents were born in the Caribbean; his mother is from Montserrat, his father from Jamaica. They learned to love winters in Canada, and for 20 years his dad made an ice rink in the backyard of their Toronto home. Subban's dad was a teacher, and he always made sure his kids understood the value of education as well as sports. Subban has two older sisters who became teachers, and his younger brothers, Malcolm and Jordan, have both been drafted into the NHL.

As a boy, P.K. — which stands for Pernell Karl — played on a novice team with Steven Stamkos and was friends with future NHL star John Tavares. In 2008 and 2009 he won gold medals playing for Canada at the World Junior Championships; he didn't see much action in 2008, but he was a key member of Team Canada in 2009 and was named to the tournament's All-Star Team.

Subban had been drafted by Montreal in 2007, but it took him a few more years to reach the NHL. He made his NHL debut during Montreal's 2009–2010 season and had a strong playoff performance that spring. By 2010–2011 he was in the NHL to stay and was one of the top rookies in the league that season. Subban won the Norris Trophy as the league's best defenceman in 2012–2013, and he was picked to play on Canada's gold medal–winning team at the 2014 Winter Olympics. Though he no longer plays for a Canadian NHL team, Subban will always have fans in Montreal.

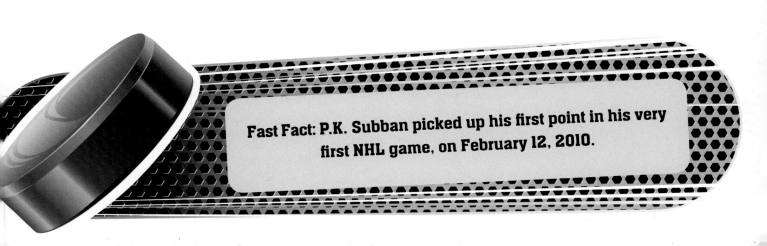

Fast Fact: P.K. Subban picked up his first point in his very first NHL game, on February 12, 2010.

MARIE-PHILIP
POULIN

LES CANADIENNES DE MONTRÉAL

Forward
Height: 1.70 m (5'7")
Weight: 76.5 kg (168 lbs.)
Born: March 28, 1991, in Beauceville, Quebec

Marie-Philip Poulin was still a teenager when people began referring to her as the Sidney Crosby of women's hockey. It was partly because she was so good so young, and partly because she had a similar style of play. "Dangerous, evasive, intelligent, passionate, difficult to knock off the puck, confident . . . and a scorer of devastating goals," said a Canadian Press story about her during the 2010 Vancouver Olympics. Poulin has very fast hands, which she credits to batting pucks out of the air with her brother, Pier-Alexandre, a college hockey player. "He helped me since I was young," said Poulin. "I owe him a lot."

Poulin began representing Canada on the international stage when she was only 16. She made her debut with the Canadian National Women's Team in an exhibition series with the Under-18 team in 2007 and played in the Under-18 Women's World Championship in 2008 and 2009. She joined the women's senior team at the 2009 World Championship. The tournament began just after her 18th birthday, making her the youngest player on the team.

Poulin was still her team's youngest player when she scored both goals in Canada's 2–0 win over the United States in the gold-medal game at the 2010 Vancouver Olympics. She was part of an even more amazing finish in the nail-biting gold-medal game at the 2014 Sochi Olympics. Canada had finally gotten on the scoreboard late in the third period, but was trailing 2–1 until Poulin got the tying goal with just 55 seconds to go. Then she scored the winning goal at 8:10 of overtime. "When people realize who I am . . . they always tell me where they were when they watched the game. It amazes me every time."

In addition to her impressive international success, Poulin has been a star player at Boston University and in the Canadian Women's Hockey League. She was CWHL Rookie of the Year in 2007–2008 and the league's leading scorer with Les Canadiennes de Montréal in 2015–2016. At only 26 years old, Poulin should be able to give her fans exciting play to watch for many more years.

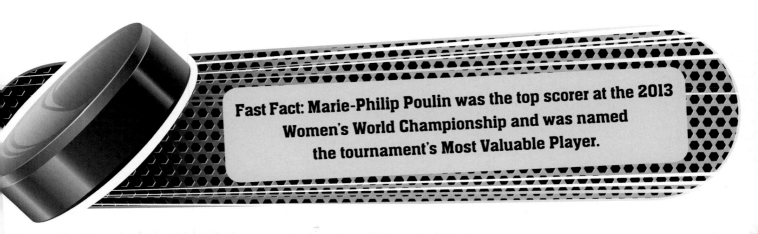

Fast Fact: Marie-Philip Poulin was the top scorer at the 2013 Women's World Championship and was named the tournament's Most Valuable Player.

JOSH DONALDSON

TORONTO BLUE JAYS

Third Base
Height: 1.85 m (6'1")
Weight: 95.5 kg (210 lbs.)
Born: December 8, 1985,
in Pensacola, Florida

Josh Donaldson has only been in Toronto since 2015, but he's already become one of the greatest players in Blue Jays history. That first year, he led Toronto into the playoffs for the first time in 22 years and was named the American League's Most Valuable Player. Donaldson is considered one of the smartest hitters in baseball. "I've been in the league for a while now. So being able to take from past experiences and know what I need to make an adjustment to get certain pitches — that's where I am today." He's also got a strong arm and is a great defensive player.

Donaldson was raised by his mother, and it was her brother — Donaldson's uncle Charlie — who discovered his hitting talent early on. Josh was about six years old the very first time he picked up the toy bat his mother had bought him. His uncle threw a few balls to him . . . and Donaldson knocked them all over the backyard! Initially though, Donaldson wanted to be a pitcher. He pitched and played shortstop for his high school in Alabama, where he was named the state's Player of the Year as a senior. When Donaldson got to university, he started playing catcher and third base, proving to be a flexible and well-rounded team member.

The Chicago Cubs drafted Donaldson as a catcher in 2007, and two years later he was traded to the Oakland Athletics. He made his major-league debut for them in 2010 behind the plate, but his big break came in 2012, when Oakland's starting third baseman hurt his knee in spring training. The A's moved Donaldson to third base, and he's been playing there ever since.

Donaldson was always a solid player in Oakland, but in the winter of 2014, the A's traded him to the Blue Jays, where he became a star. During his first season with Toronto, Donaldson hit 41 home runs and led the league with 122 runs scored and 123 runs batted in. He had another great year in 2016, leading the Blue Jays into the playoffs yet again.

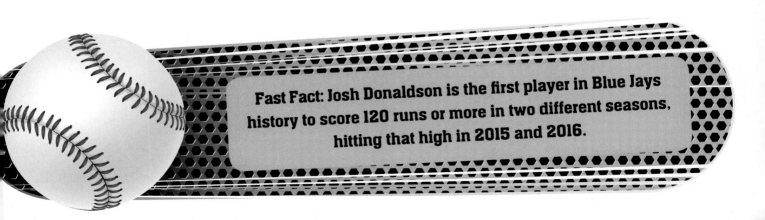

Fast Fact: Josh Donaldson is the first player in Blue Jays history to score 120 runs or more in two different seasons, hitting that high in 2015 and 2016.

JOEY
VOTTO

CINCINNATI REDS

First Base
Height: 1.88 m (6'2")
Weight: 100 kg (220 lbs.)
Born: September 10, 1983,
in Toronto, Ontario

Canadians have played on Major League Baseball teams since the 1880s, but it's always been tough to get to the show. With our short summers and long winters, it's hard to get as much baseball practice as players from countries farther south. To make it to the majors, Canadian players need to give it their all . . . and maybe a little bit more. It also helps if you have a great batting eye like Joey Votto.

Votto was born in Toronto and grew up in Etobicoke, where he played both baseball and basketball in high school. His father was a big baseball fan, and together they watched Canadian sluggers Larry Walker and Justin Morneau make a name for themselves in the majors during the 1990s and 2000s. Joey wanted to be like them. In 2002, Votto was drafted by the Cincinnati Reds, and he spent five years in their minor-league system before making his major-league debut on September 4, 2007. By the next season he was the Reds' regular first baseman.

With his great eye at the plate, Votto always draws a lot of walks and can usually be found among baseball's leaders in batting average and on-base percentage. In 2008, Votto led all National League rookies in hitting (.297), home runs (24) and several other categories. His 84 RBI broke the Reds' rookie record set by Hall of Famer Frank Robinson.

Sadly, Votto's father died suddenly that same summer. The loss hit him hard. Even though he missed about a month of the 2009 season dealing with his depression over his father, Votto had another great year. Then in 2010, Votto led Cincinnati to the playoffs for the first time in 15 years. He hit .324 that season with 37 homers and 113 RBIs and was named the National League's MVP. "I couldn't help but cry," Votto said, "because I know how much this would have meant to my father." He also won the Lou Marsh Trophy as Canada's Athlete of the Year. In 2012, Votto signed a new contract extension with the Reds worth $251 million over 12 seasons. It made him the highest-paid Canadian athlete in history. Sometimes big money leads to big pressure, but Votto has continued to put up big numbers, finishing the 2016 season with a hot streak after the All-Star break, during which he batted .408!

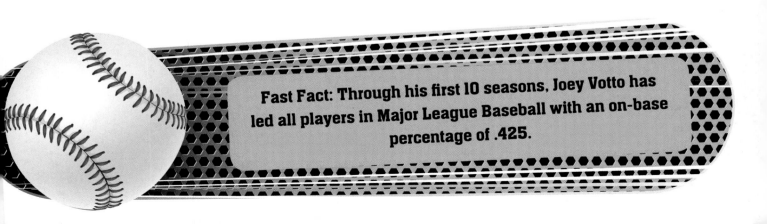

Fast Fact: Through his first 10 seasons, Joey Votto has led all players in Major League Baseball with an on-base percentage of .425.

MIKE TROUT

LOS ANGELES ANGELS

**Centre Field
Height: 1.88 m (6'2")
Weight: 107 kg (235 lbs.)
Born: August 7, 1991, in
Vineland, New Jersey**

Baseball people love to compare current players to former stars . . . and when it comes to Mike Trout, he gets compared to some pretty amazing ones. In 2012, a *Sports Illustrated* writer called Trout "the best young player in baseball since Ted Williams," the baseball legend who hit .406 in 1941. Trout's often compared to Mickey Mantle, the great New York Yankees slugger who hit some of the longest home runs in baseball history. Like Mantle, Trout can hit home runs, steal bases and make great plays in centre field. In 2015, Trout became the youngest player ever to reach 100 home runs and 100 steals.

Mike Trout was mainly a shortstop when he started playing baseball as a boy.

In high school, he was a pitcher and a shortstop until he switched to centre field in grade twelve. That's when scouts really started to notice him. Given how great he's become, it's hard to believe that Trout didn't get selected by the Los Angeles Angels until the 25th pick in the 2009 MLB Draft. Then again, he was only 17 years old.

"The first couple of years in the minors were tough for me," Trout remembers. "My numbers were there, but being away from home so young was tough." He wasn't in the minors very long. Trout was only 19 when he made his debut with the Angels in 2011, and a year later he was in the major leagues to stay. In 2012, Trout hit .326 and led the American League with 49 stolen bases and 129 runs scored. He was named the American League Rookie of the Year and finished second in voting for the American League MVP Award.

Trout went on to win the MVP Award twice — in 2014 and in 2016 — and has been among the top vote-getters every season he's played. He also always ranks among the leaders in a statistic known as WAR — wins above replacement — which measures a player's total value to his team by calculating how many more wins he's worth compared to an average player at his position. At 48.5, Trout's career WAR is already shaping up to be one of the highest in baseball history.

Fast Fact: In his first five full seasons, Mike Trout led the American League in runs scored four times — and led the entire major leagues three times.

JOSÉ
ALTUVE

HOUSTON ASTROS

Second Base
Height: 1.68 m (5'6")
Weight: 75 kg (165 lbs.)
Born: May 6, 1990, in Maracay, Venezuela

When José Altuve was 16, he attended a tryout for the Houston Astros in his native Venezuela, but he got sent home because he was too short. His father convinced him to go back to the tryout the next day. This time Altuve impressed the Astros evaluators. They gave him a contract with a small signing bonus of $15,000. It turned out to be one of the best bargains in baseball because Altuve now has one of the game's highest batting averages!

Altuve is still short. At 1.68 metres (5 feet, 6 inches), he's one of the shortest players in baseball today — and of all time. But he has quick reflexes and tremendous hand-eye coordination. He's able to hit balls no matter how they are pitched: high, low, inside, outside, fast or slow. Playing in the minor leagues for Houston in 2011, Altuve had a .408 batting average in Class-A baseball. That earned him a promotion to Double A. When he hit .361 there, the Astros decided to skip Triple A and bring him straight up to the major leagues. He made his debut in Houston on July 20, 2011, and got a hit in each of his first seven games.

In 2012, his first full season with the Astros, Altuve hit .290 and had 33 stolen bases. He hit .283 with 35 steals in 2013, but he wasn't satisfied. He felt he had to get himself in better shape. Before the 2014 season, Altuve dedicated himself to an improved diet and more physical fitness. He also worked hard at spring training to make adjustments to his swing.

The results were amazing! Altuve led the majors by a mile with 225 hits and a .341 batting average. "I think I was able to see the ball better and hit the ball harder," Altuve said. "I think that was the key for this year." He also led the American League with 56 stolen bases. Altuve won a second American League batting title in 2016 when he hit .338. Houston used to be one of the worst teams in baseball, but now, armed with one of the game's most exciting players, they are always a contender in the playoff hunt.

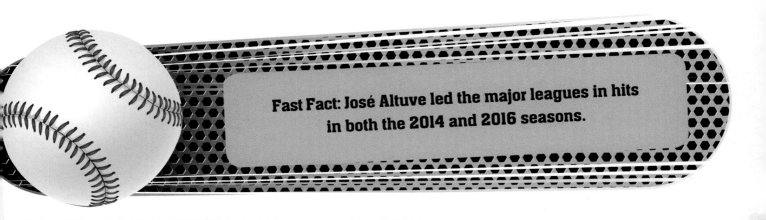

Fast Fact: José Altuve led the major leagues in hits in both the 2014 and 2016 seasons.

CLAYTON KERSHAW

LOS ANGELES DODGERS

Pitcher
Height: 1.93 m (6'4")
Weight: 102 kg (225 lbs.)
Born: March 19, 1988, in Dallas, Texas

Baseball's best pitchers are usually tall and strong, but when Clayton Kershaw started high school, he was short and out of shape. By grade twelve, he'd shot up to his adult height and become a strike-throwing machine. The Los Angeles Dodgers chose the strong left-hander with the seventh pick in the first round of the 2006 MLB Draft. Kershaw raced through the minor leagues, piling up strikeouts along the way. He was only 20 years old when he made his major-league debut in 2008, and he struck out the first batter he faced.

Kershaw was just a few weeks past his 21st birthday when he struck out 13 San Francisco Giants on April 15, 2009. That made him the youngest Dodger to strike out so many in one game since legendary lefty Sandy Koufax in 1955. Koufax was probably the best pitcher in baseball in the early 1960s, and Kershaw soon became the best pitcher in the game today.

In 2011, Kershaw won the National League Cy Young Award for the first time. He led the league with 21 wins, 248 strikeouts and a 2.28 earned run average (ERA), making him the first Dodgers pitcher since Koufax in 1966 to lead the league in the three main "triple crown" categories.

Kershaw went on to become the first pitcher in baseball history to lead the major leagues in ERA for four consecutive seasons, capping off the streak in 2014 when he had a truly amazing year. That season, Kershaw had a 1.77 ERA and posted a record of 21–3, even though he missed the first month with an injury and only pitched 27 games. He also threw a no-hitter that year, and not only did he win his third Cy Young Award, he became the first National League pitcher since 1968 to win the MVP Award.

In 2015, Kershaw became the first pitcher in 13 years to top the 300-strikeout mark when he led the major leagues with 301. Injuries cut into another great season in 2016, but Kershaw proved he could still dominate batters when he came back strong in the playoffs.

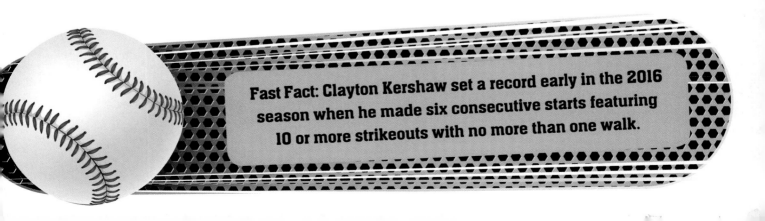

Fast Fact: Clayton Kershaw set a record early in the 2016 season when he made six consecutive starts featuring 10 or more strikeouts with no more than one walk.

DEMAR
DEROZAN

TORONTO RAPTORS

Guard
Height: 2.01 m (6'7")
Weight: 100 kg (220 lbs.)
Born: August 7, 1989, in Compton, California

DeMar DeRozan was in grade six the first time he dunked a basketball — and he's been known for his high-flying dunks ever since. DeRozan made the Compton High School team in grade nine and quickly attracted national attention. By the time he was in grade twelve, DeRozan wasn't just earning All-Star awards in Los Angeles and California, but All-American honours too. He began his career with the University of Southern California in 2008. DeRozan played every game for USC that season and had one of the best freshman years in the school's history.

After just one year of university, DeRozan entered the 2009 NBA Draft. His mother suffers from a serious disease known as lupus, and DeRozan knew that the money he would earn as a professional would help her get the best medical care possible. The Toronto Raptors selected DeRozan with the ninth pick in the draft. He established himself as one of the NBA's rising young stars during his first four seasons with the Raptors, but the team didn't do so well in those years. Then, in 2013–2014, things began to turn around for DeRozan and the Raptors. He led the team in scoring with 22.7 points per game and earned a spot in the NBA All-Star Game. Toronto hadn't made the playoffs for five years, but they made the playoffs that year . . . and in every season since! DeRozan has also used his on-court success to give back, partnering with Lupus Canada to raise awareness for the disease.

DeRozan had another great year with the Raptors in 2015–2016. He ranked among the NBA scoring leaders with 23.5 points per game and appeared in his second All-Star Game, in front of cheering hometown fans. DeRozan also won a gold medal playing for Team USA, alongside his Raptors teammate and friend Kyle Lowry, at the 2016 Olympics in Rio de Janeiro. DeRozan then rode his gold-medal high into the start of the Raptors' 2016–2017 season. "He is playing at another level right now," said Raptors point guard Kyle Lowry after a sizzling performance against the Washington Wizards. "He's saving possessions, he's creating possessions, he's creating offence and tonight he hit a three."

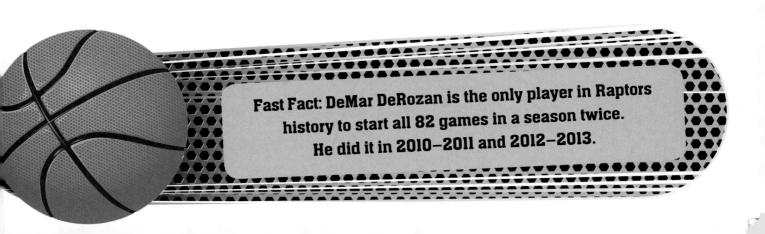

Fast Fact: DeMar DeRozan is the only player in Raptors history to start all 82 games in a season twice. He did it in 2010–2011 and 2012–2013.

ANDREW WIGGINS

MINNESOTA TIMBERWOLVES

Forward
Height: 2.03 m (6'8")
Weight: 90.5 kg (199 lbs.)
Born: February 23, 1995,
in Thornhill, Ontario

Andrew Wiggins is a rising star from a family of impressive athletes. His father, Mitchell, played in the NBA between 1983 and 1992. His mother, Marita, was a sprinter who won two silver medals for Canada at the 1984 Summer Olympics, and his older brother Nick also plays professional basketball.

At age nine, Andrew Wiggins was already 1.70 metres (5 feet, 7 inches) tall and playing organized basketball in Toronto. His talent was obvious, and after his first practice, his coach predicted that in another ten years Wiggins would be a first-round pick in the NBA Draft. By the time Wiggins was 14 years old, he was 1.98 metres (6 feet, 6 inches) tall. He played his first two years of high school basketball at Vaughan Secondary School just outside of Toronto, but in 2011 he moved to a school in West Virginia. In his final year of high school, Wiggins earned all sorts of national attention in the United States and was the first Canadian to be named the Gatorade National Player of the Year, an award given to the top high school player in the United States. In 2013–2014 he played college ball for the University of Kansas and was practically a human highlight reel, setting many freshman scoring records.

"No one's game is perfect," Wiggins said after his season in Kansas. "I know I have a lot I have to improve on." Even so, he decided to leave university for the NBA. Wiggins was picked in the first round of the 2014 NBA Draft, just like his coach had predicted . . . and he was the first overall pick!

The Cleveland Cavaliers drafted Wiggins, but then they traded him to the Minnesota Timberwolves. Minnesota had a very weak team, but that gave Wiggins a lot of opportunities to play. He was on the court for every single game with the Timberwolves in 2014–2015, and he led all NBA rookies in scoring. To no one's surprise, Wiggins was named the league's Rookie of the Year — the first Canadian ever to win the award.

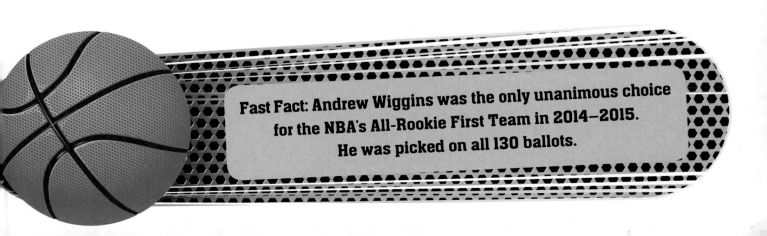

Fast Fact: Andrew Wiggins was the only unanimous choice for the NBA's All-Rookie First Team in 2014–2015. He was picked on all 130 ballots.

LEBRON
JAMES

CLEVELAND CAVALIERS

Forward
Height: 2.03 m (6'8")
Weight: 113.5 kg (250 lbs.)
Born: December 30, 1984,
in Akron, Ohio

LeBron James has always been loyal to his hometown roots. James comes from Akron, Ohio, less than an hour away from Cleveland. He showed his tremendous athletic promise early on, and when he was nine years old, James moved in with the family of a local youth football coach. The coach introduced him to basketball to keep him busy during the football off-season, and James had fun playing with his new friends. They promised to stick together and chose to attend Akron's St. Vincent-St. Mary High School, a school with a strong basketball program.

James made the varsity team when he was in grade nine and led the school to three state championships in four seasons.

He was so good, and his games were so popular, that they sometimes played at the University of Akron so that more people could see him play. By the time James was in grade twelve, there was so much interest in him all across the United States that a cable company offered his high school games in a pay-per-view package. LeBron didn't play university basketball — he went straight to the 2003 NBA Draft instead. The Cleveland Cavaliers had the first pick and were thrilled to get a homegrown young superstar. In his very first game, James scored 25 points — the most ever for an NBA player straight out of high school.

From the 2003–2004 season to 2009–2010, James ranked among the league's top scorers as he took the Cavaliers from being one of the worst teams in basketball to one of the best. But then he shocked the fans in Cleveland when he left to join the Miami Heat. Teamed with other superstars in Miami, James played four seasons with the Heat and won back-to-back NBA championships in 2011–2012 and 2012–2013.

After the 2013–2014 season, James decided to come home to Cleveland. "I came back for a reason," he would say. "To bring a championship to our city." No Cleveland team had won a title in any sport since 1964, but in his second season back in town, James — true to his word! — delivered the city the 2016 NBA championship.

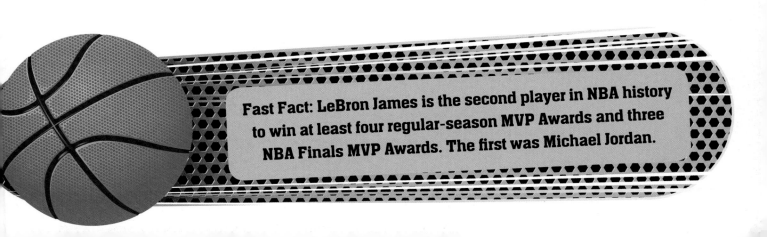

Fast Fact: LeBron James is the second player in NBA history to win at least four regular-season MVP Awards and three NBA Finals MVP Awards. The first was Michael Jordan.

STEPHEN
CURRY

GOLDEN STATE WARRIORS

Guard
Height: 1.90 m (6'3")
Weight: 86.5 kg (190 lbs.)
Born: March 14, 1988,
in Akron, Ohio

With the average height in the NBA listed as 2.01 metres (6 feet, 7 inches), Stephen Curry is on the smaller side for a basketball player, at just 1.91 metres (6 feet, 3 inches). Then again, size doesn't matter much when you're one of the greatest shooters in basketball history!

Curry is the son of former NBA player Dell Curry, who played for the Raptors from 1999 to 2002. The family lived in Etobicoke, Ontario, in 2002 and Stephen went to Queensway Christian College for grade eight. He led their basketball team to an undefeated season, and that same year he was also on the Toronto 5-0 rep team that played games all across Ontario. Led by Curry, the Toronto 5-0 team handed the Scarborough Blues — at that time featuring future Canadian NBA stars Kelly Olynyk

and Cory Joseph — one of their only losses of the season.

When Curry's father retired, the family moved back to North Carolina. Stephen continued to excel at his game and attended Davidson College. In his third season at the school, in 2008–2009, Curry led all of college basketball in scoring, with 28.6 points per game. He decided to leave school before his final season and was chosen by the Golden State Warriors with the seventh pick in the 2009 NBA Draft. It took Curry a few years to make his mark in professional basketball, but his unique skills soon began to pay off.

Curry has perfected his shot from behind the NBA's three-point line. In fact, he's so good at it that he's changed the risky three-point shot into a key offensive weapon. He set a new record in 2012–2013 when he made 272 three-pointers, and then broke it when he made 286 three-point shots in 2014–2015. That season Curry also led Golden State to the NBA championship and was named the league's Most Valuable Player.

He was even better in 2015–2016, shattering his own record by making 402 three-pointers and leading the NBA in scoring, with an average of 30.1 points per game. Golden State won more games than anyone in league history with a record of 73–9, led by his unstoppable talent. Curry started the 2016–2017 season by breaking his own record, sinking 13 three-pointers in a single game, again leading his team into victory.

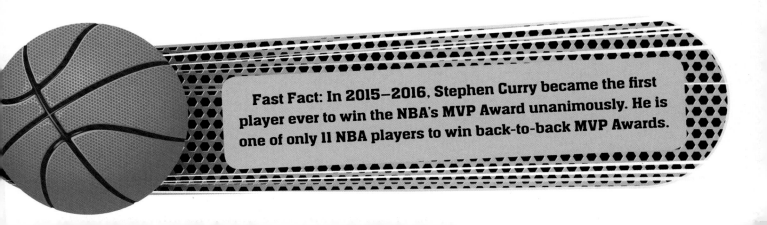

Fast Fact: In 2015–2016, Stephen Curry became the first player ever to win the NBA's MVP Award unanimously. He is one of only 11 NBA players to win back-to-back MVP Awards.

RUSSELL WESTBROOK

OKLAHOMA CITY THUNDER

Guard
Height: 1.90 m (6'3")
Weight: 91 kg (200 lbs.)
Born: November 12, 1988,
in Long Beach, California

Russell Westbrook was struck by a terrible loss early in his life, but he turned it into an inspiration. When Westbrook started playing high school basketball near Los Angeles, California, his best friend, Khelcey Barrs III, was the star of the team. Westbrook and Barrs hoped to go to the same university, but Barrs was the one getting all the best offers. Then tragedy struck. During a pickup game, Barrs collapsed and died of a heart condition. Westbrook had always been a hard worker, but now he worked harder than ever. He was determined to honour his friend by living out their dream.

Westbrook became the star of his high school team in grade twelve and earned a scholarship to UCLA, a college with a legendary basketball program. He played two years at UCLA and then entered the 2008 NBA Draft. Westbrook wasn't a big scorer, but he was a great defensive player and the Seattle Supersonics chose him fourth overall in the draft. A few days later, the team was moved to a new city, and suddenly Westbrook was a member of the Oklahoma City Thunder.

Westbrook had a good rookie season in 2008–2009 and has just kept getting better and better. He earned All-NBA Second Team honours four times in five years from 2010 to 2015, and he was selected to the All-NBA First Team for the first time in 2015–2016. He's on the short side for a pro basketball player, but Westbrook makes up for it by being one of the best athletes in the NBA. He scored a career-high 54 points on April 12, 2015. He led the NBA in scoring during the 2014–2015 season, with an average of 28.1 points per game.

Westbrook plays an intense, fast-paced game that often makes it hard for his opponents to keep up. He is a high scorer who can also dish the ball effectively to his teammates to set them up for shots. And in every game he plays Westbrook wears a KB3 wristband to honour his best friend, Khelcey Barrs III.

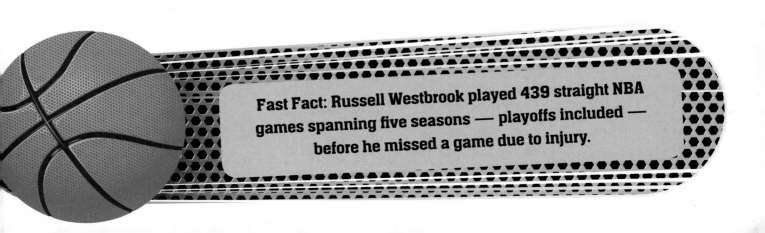

Fast Fact: Russell Westbrook played 439 straight NBA games spanning five seasons — playoffs included — before he missed a game due to injury.

MIKE REILLY

Quarterback
Height: 1.90 m (6'3")
Weight: 104.5 kg (230 lbs.)
Born: January 25, 1985,
in Kennewick, Washington

Mike Reilly joined some of the greatest quarterbacks in Canadian football history when he passed for more than 5,000 yards in 2016. The road to success in the CFL hasn't been a smooth one, but Reilly never gave up. At 1.90 metres (6 feet, 3 inches) and 104.5 kilograms (230 pounds), he certainly had the size to succeed as a quarterback, but getting the opportunity to prove himself wasn't always easy. When he finally got his chance with the Edmonton Eskimos, Reilly became a star.

A native of Kennewick, Washington, Reilly hoped to be the quarterback at Washington State University, but he barely got a look. After sitting out an entire season, he decided to transfer to Central Washington University, a smaller school playing in a different division of American college football. Reilly played in 46 games over four seasons at Central Washington and set a college football record by throwing at least one touchdown pass in every single game. He completed over 64 percent of his passes in college, and threw for more than 12,000 yards, but he wasn't drafted by the NFL.

Reilly signed with the CFL's BC Lions in 2010. He played a little bit, but the Lions didn't give Reilly much of a chance. Still, the Edmonton Eskimos liked what they saw and traded for him in 2013. "This is a step toward stabilizing our quarterback position," said Eskimos general manager Ed Hervey. "Mike has the chance to be an elite quarterback in this league." Hervey was right! In 2013 Reilly was second in the CFL with 4,207 passing yards and led all quarterbacks with 709 rushing yards. Injuries slowed him down over the next two seasons, but after returning to action in late 2015, Reilly led the Eskimos to eight straight wins. Edmonton finished the season 14–4 for the best record in the CFL. In the playoffs, the Eskimos knocked off their biggest rivals, the Calgary Stampeders, in the West Division Final, and then faced the Ottawa Redblacks for the Grey Cup. Edmonton won the game 26–20 and Reilly was named the Most Valuable Player.

Fast Fact: Mike Reilly passed for a career-high 511 yards on August 18, 2013. That's the fourth-highest single-game total in Edmonton Eskimos history.

CAM NEWTON

CAROLINA PANTHERS

Quarterback
Height: 1.95 m (6'5")
Weight: 111.5 kg (245 lbs.)
Born: May 11, 1989,
in Atlanta, Georgia

Cam Newton is the greatest combination of passer and runner the NFL has ever seen. Cameron Jerrell "Cam" Newton has two brothers and was raised in a home that valued education, hard work and athletics. His mother, Jackie, helped the boys keep up with their homework, and their father, Cecil, kept them busy with football, part-time jobs and a lot of chores.

This dedication to hard work paid off; Cam was a standout by the time he was 16, quarterbacking for his high school team. But when he began his college career at the University of Florida in 2007, Newton didn't get to play much, so he transferred to Auburn University in 2010. That season, Newton threw for nearly 3,000 yards and ran for over 1,400. Auburn went 12–0 in the regular season, won its conference championship, and then won the National Championship Game. Newton earned many honours for his play, including the Heisman Trophy as the most outstanding player in college football.

No player since 1950 had won the Heisman Trophy, led his team to the national championship, and then been picked first in the following year's NFL Draft — until the Carolina Panthers took Newton first overall in 2011. In his rookie season he became the first quarterback to throw for 400 yards in his very first game. He was also the first rookie to reach 4,000 yards in passing in one season and the first rookie quarterback to rush for more than 700 yards. In 2015, Newton was the first NFL player to pass for at least 30 touchdowns — he threw for 35 — and run for 10 in the same season.

"I don't view myself as a quarterback," Newton told the *Players' Tribune* in 2016. He sees himself as a football player. Critics have often wondered how long Newton will be able to last playing the all-out style he does, but Newton isn't worried. "I'm really willing to do anything to win a football game. Running, throwing, blocking, catching . . . Anything."

With Newton, the Panthers quickly went from being the NFL's worst team to one of its best. In 2015, Carolina went 15–1 in the regular season and Newton was named the league's Most Valuable Player.

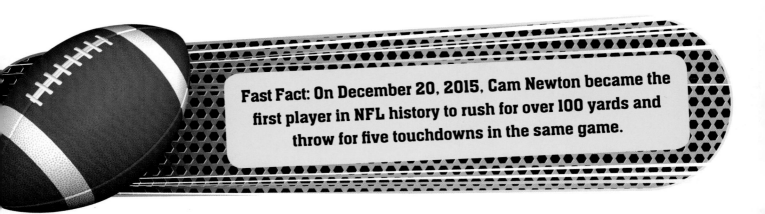

Fast Fact: On December 20, 2015, Cam Newton became the first player in NFL history to rush for over 100 yards and throw for five touchdowns in the same game.

TOM BRADY

Quarterback
Height: 1.93 m (6'4")
Weight: 102 kg (225 lbs.)
Born: August 3, 1977,
in San Mateo, California

Growing up, Tom Brady was a big fan of the San Francisco 49ers and went to lots of their games with his father. At that time, the 49ers were the NFL's best team, and their quarterback, Joe Montana, was his idol. Montana led the 49ers to four Super Bowl championships and Brady has grown up to match his hero by winning the Super Bowl four times . . . and counting!

Tom Brady played football, basketball and baseball in high school. He was good enough at baseball that in 1995 he was drafted by the Montreal Expos (who later moved and became the Washington Nationals), but Brady wanted to play football. He went to the University of Michigan, but barely played at all his first two years there. Brady won the starter's job in his third year, but he had to battle hard to keep it in his fourth season. He went on to lead Michigan to an exciting victory in the 2000 Orange Bowl in the final game of his college career.

For someone who's become one of the greatest quarterbacks in history, Brady didn't attract much interest after he finished university. New England finally took him with the 199th pick in the 2000 NFL Draft, and he started that year as the Patriots' fourth-string quarterback. He made it into just one game and completed only one pass. Then, early in the 2001 season, New England's starting quarterback was injured. Brady took over and led the Patriots to 11 wins in 14 games. They won three more games in the playoffs, including the Super Bowl, and Brady has been the team's top quarterback ever since.

For much of his career, Brady vied with Peyton Manning to be considered the NFL's best quarterback. Manning often had more impressive statistics, but Brady's team won more championships. No quarterback has ever led his team to more division titles or appeared in the Super Bowl more times than Brady has, and Brady and his childhood hero Joe Montana are the only players in NFL history to be named the Super Bowl MVP three times.

Fast Fact: In 2007, Tom Brady became the first quarterback in NFL history to throw 50 touchdown passes in one season.

ADAM BIGHILL

BC LIONS

Linebacker
Height: 1.78 m (5'10")
Weight: 104.5 kg (230 lbs.)
Born: October 16, 1988,
in Montesano, Washington

Adam Bighill is an all-important linchpin for his team now, and known for his success on the field, but things were not always easy for him. He was born with a birth defect known as a bilateral cleft lip and palate, and when he was a boy, other children would make fun of his appearance. Bighill used these early challenges to fuel his dream of playing professional football. Today, he is a CFL star and works with a charity called Making Faces, which helps kids with facial differences cope with shyness and bullying.

Bighill grew up in Montesano, Washington, and began playing football when he was just seven years old. He later attended Central Washington University, where he played two seasons with future Edmonton Eskimos quarterback Mike Reilly. In his first three years at Central Washington, Bighill wore number 41. In 2010, his final season, he was given number 44, which Central Washington reserves for star defensive players who display toughness, discipline and tenacity. Bighill wears number 44 with the BC Lions to this day.

Following university, the Lions signed Bighill, who had impressed them with his skills at a free agent tryout camp in the spring of 2011. As a rookie in 2011, he earned more and more playing time as the season progressed and was a regular on the starting defence over the last seven games of the season. In the playoffs, he helped the Lions win the Grey Cup. Heading into the 2012 season, Bighill won the position of the Lions' starting middle linebacker and was excited about what he could do. "I want to be a guy who's known as consistent at doing his job all the time," he said, "and when those big plays come, I'm going to make them." Bighill has certainly done that, earning a spot on the West Division All-Star Team in 2012, 2013, 2014 and 2015 and on the CFL All-Star Team in 2012, 2013 and 2015.

Bighill and his teammate Solomon Elimimian — who has set many of his own records — give the Lions the two best linebackers in the CFL. In 2015, Bighill had his best season ever, leading the CFL with 114 defensive tackles, and winning the award for Most Outstanding Defensive Player.

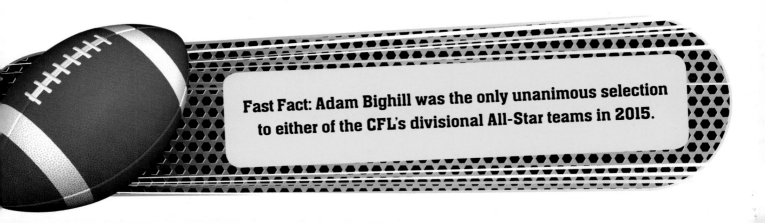

Fast Fact: Adam Bighill was the only unanimous selection to either of the CFL's divisional All-Star teams in 2015.

JULIO JONES

ATLANTA FALCONS

Wide Receiver
Height: 1.90 m (6'3")
Weight: 100 kg (220 lbs.)
Born: February 3, 1989,
in Foley, Alabama

In 2015, Julio Jones had one of the greatest seasons any wide receiver has ever had. He caught 136 passes, tying him with Pittsburgh's Antonio Brown for the second-most catches ever in an NFL season. His total of 1,871 single-season receiving yards is the second highest of all time. So it was no surprise that he got to play in the Pro Bowl for the third time in his career. He also earned his very first selection to the NFL First-Team All-Pro roster.

Jones — whose actual first name is Quintorris — was born in Foley, Alabama, and went to Foley High School. In addition to football, Jones played on his school's basketball team and was an outstanding track and field athlete. He was the Alabama high school champion in long jump, triple jump and high jump, but football was still his best sport. In his last year of high school, in 2007–2008, he was considered the best high school receiver in the United States and was ranked as the top high school player by *Sports Illustrated* magazine.

He then attended the University of Alabama and quickly became a star there too. Jones was the first freshman wide receiver to be the team's opening day starter and went on to be named Freshman of the Year in the Southeastern Conference. He slumped at the start of his second season, but came on strong as the year went along and helped Alabama win the national championship. He set a school record the next season with 78 catches, but then decided to leave Alabama and enter the 2011 NFL Draft. The Atlanta Falcons chose him with the sixth overall pick.

In Atlanta, Jones has become one of the most explosive receivers in the NFL. He led the NFL in 2015 with an average of 116.9 receiving yards per game. That's the seventh-highest single-season average in league history. He's always a threat to score long touchdowns. "To me, he's good at so many things," says his former teammate Roddy White. "He's able to run. He's big. He's strong . . . He doesn't have really any weaknesses in his game."

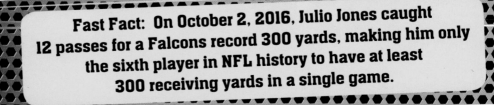

Fast Fact: On October 2, 2016, Julio Jones caught 12 passes for a Falcons record 300 yards, making him only the sixth player in NFL history to have at least 300 receiving yards in a single game.

JULIAN
DE GUZMAN

OTTAWA FURY

Midfielder
Height: 1.70 m (5'7")
Weight: 72 kg (158 lbs.)
Born: March 25, 1981,
in Scarborough, Ontario

Soccer is the world's most popular game, and the amount of talent needed to play internationally is intense. Julian de Guzman is one of a handful of Canadians to break into this level. He was just the third Canadian ever to play in the German First Bundesliga (the top league in Germany), in 2002, and was the first Canadian to play in La Liga (the top league in Spain), in 2005. Talent runs in the family; his younger brother, Jonathan, also plays professional soccer in Europe. De Guzman made his debut for the Canadian Men's National Team in 2002 and is now its captain. He has represented Canada in more international soccer games than any other man, surpassing the previous record of 84 matches in 2015.

Julian de Guzman was born and raised in Scarborough, Ontario. He started playing with the Wexford Soccer Club when he was five years old. As an 18-year-old, de Guzman made his debut with the Canadian youth program, and in 2001 he represented Canada at the Under-20 World Cup in Argentina. He began playing soccer in Europe in 2000, but came home to Toronto in 2009 when he signed with Toronto FC.

He didn't have much success in Toronto at first, and he was traded to FC Dallas in 2012. He then left to play in Germany and Greece in 2013 and 2014, but returned to Canada in 2015 and is now the captain of the Ottawa Fury in the North American Soccer League. During the 2016 season, de Guzman was one of 12 Canadian players with the Fury — which had more home-grown talent than any other Canadian soccer team. "Many Canadians who follow soccer, whether it is NASL or MLS, enjoy seeing a Canadian club playing," de Guzman said, "[but] seeing a club giving the chance to local talents will definitely help the game grow in this country."

De Guzman has represented Canada in many CONCACAF Gold Cup games. (CONCACAF is the group that oversees soccer in North America, Central America and the Caribbean.) He was an All-Star and the tournament MVP at the 2007 Gold Cup and an All-Star and the Canadian MVP in 2013.

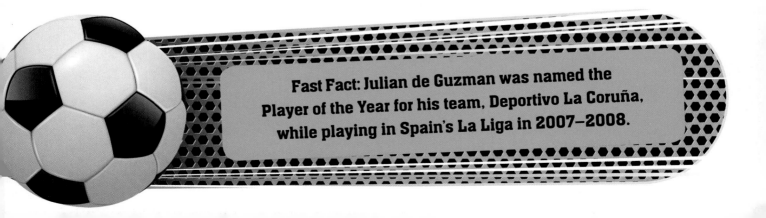

Fast Fact: Julian de Guzman was named the Player of the Year for his team, Deportivo La Coruña, while playing in Spain's La Liga in 2007–2008.

LIONEL MESSI

FC BARCELONA

Forward
Height: 1.70 m (5'7")
Weight: 72 kg (159 lbs.)
Born: June 24, 1987,
in Rosario, Argentina

Many fans and experts alike consider Lionel Messi to be the greatest soccer player in the world. Some believe he's the greatest of all time. Messi holds several major scoring records, and he has led his club team — FC Barcelona of Spain's La Liga — to all sorts of titles. Messi seems to move faster than everyone else on the soccer pitch, and his skill with the ball makes him hard to stop.

Messi began playing at age six with Argentina's famous Newell's Old Boys organization and quickly became a young star, small as he was. Five years later he was diagnosed with a rare health condition in which his body wasn't growing properly. When Messi was 13, he moved to Spain because FC Barcelona had agreed to cover all expenses for his medical treatment. Messi joined Barcelona's youth academy, and after a year of being treated for his disease, he began to play for Barcelona's youth club in 2002–2003. He scored 36 goals in 30 games that season, playing on what became known as the "Baby Dream Team." The next year, Messi began moving up the ranks of the Barcelona organization. He made his debut with the men's team on November 16, 2003, when he was just 16 years old. A year later, at 17, he became the youngest player ever to represent FC Barcelona in an official competition. On June 24, 2005, Messi signed his first contract as an official member of the men's team.

Over the years, Messi has led FC Barcelona to eight La Liga championships and four UEFA (European) Champions League titles. In the 2006 World Cup, he became the youngest player to represent Argentina, at age 18. He has yet to win that prestigious tournament, but he did win an Olympic gold medal in 2008. Individually, Messi has won the Ballon d'Or as soccer's player of the year a record five times, including the 2015 honours. In 2016, Messi was breaking more all-time records — some of them already his own — including most hat tricks in the Champions League and most goals in Champions League group stage games.

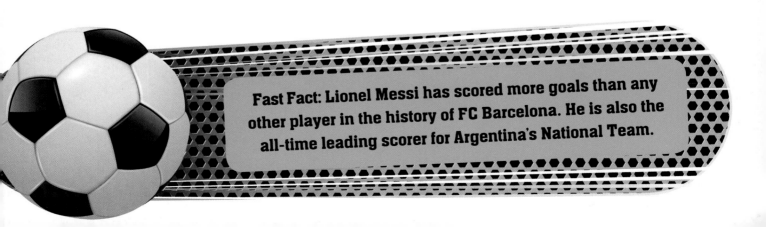

Fast Fact: Lionel Messi has scored more goals than any other player in the history of FC Barcelona. He is also the all-time leading scorer for Argentina's National Team.

CRISTIANO
RONALDO

REAL MADRID

Forward
Height: 1.85 m (6'1")
Weight: 80 kg (176 lbs.)
Born: February 5, 1985,
in Funchal, Portugal

Those who don't think Lionel Messi is the greatest player in soccer today are likely to choose Cristiano Ronaldo of Portugal (not be confused with former Brazilian soccer star Ronaldo) instead. Ronaldo is the only four-time winner of the European Golden Shoe Award as the top scorer in Europe. In 2015, he was named the best Portuguese player of all time by the Portuguese Football Federation during its 100th anniversary celebration.

Cristiano Ronaldo dos Santos Aveiro began playing soccer as a child with CF Andorinha. His father was the team's equipment manager. When he was 12, Ronaldo moved closer to Portugal's capital Lisbon in order to join the youth academy at Sporting CP. He made his first appearance with Sporting's men's team when he was 16, and a year later, on October 7, 2002, he made his debut for Sporting in the Primeira Liga, Portugal's top league.

During the 2002–2003 season, Sporting played a game against Manchester United, the legendary English soccer team. Ronaldo led Sporting to a 3–1 victory, and the Manchester players were so impressed they urged their manager, Sir Alex Ferguson, to sign him — which he did. "He is an extremely talented footballer," said Ferguson. "He's one of the most exciting young players I've ever seen." Ronaldo joined Manchester United for the 2003–2004 season. He helped his new team win England's FA Cup final that season, and he went on to win the Ballon d'Or in 2008. Ronaldo remained with Manchester United until the 2009–2010 season, and then joined Real Madrid in Spain's La Liga. It cost his new team a record sum of 94 million Euros (over $145 million Canadian) to buy Ronaldo's contract. With Real Madrid, Ronaldo won the league championship in 2011–2012 and earned the coveted Ballon d'Or in 2013 and 2014.

In international competition, Ronaldo has represented Portugal in over 130 games, which is a national record. He's played at the World Cup in 2006, 2010 and 2014, and in 2016 he led Portugal to the UEFA European Championship (or Euro) title.

Fast Fact: Cristiano Ronaldo won three straight English Premier League championships with Manchester United (2007 to 2009) and holds the record for scoring the most hat tricks in Spain's La Liga.

PAUL POGBA

MANCHESTER UNITED

Midfielder
Height: 1.90 m (6'3")
Weight: 80 kg (176 lbs.)
Born: March 15, 1993,
in Lagny-sur-Marne, France

During the summer of 2016, Paul Pogba became the most expensive soccer player in the world. His former team, Manchester United, paid a whopping 105 million Euros (around $153 million Canadian) to transfer him back from Juventus in Italy. Pogba is one of the most dynamic players in the game today, known for his energy and his explosive playing style. He's tall and, with his long legs, Italian fans called him *Il Polpo Paul* — Paul the Octopus.

Paul Pogba was born in France to parents who'd emigrated from Guinea. He has two older brothers who also play pro soccer.

Pogba began playing for a youth team near his hometown when he was only six years old. When he was 14, he was spotted by the pro team Le Havre and joined their youth system. In 2008, Pogba was named captain of both Le Havre's Under-16 team and France's Under-16 National Team.

His play was so good that it attracted the attention of some of the most famous teams in Europe, and in 2009 Pogba joined the youth team at Manchester United. He became a regular member of the men's team in 2011, but left to join Juventus the following season.

During Pogba's four years in Serie A (the top league in Italy), Juventus won the championship every season. They also reached the UEFA Champions League final in 2015, but lost to Lionel Messi's FC Barcelona.

In international play, Pogba represented France at different youth levels between 2008 and 2013. He made his debut for the French National Team in 2013, and a year later he was playing for France at the 2014 World Cup. Les Bleus, as the team is known, reached the quarter-finals and Pogba was named the tournament's Best Young Player. At the 2016 UEFA European Championship, Pogba helped France reach the championship game.

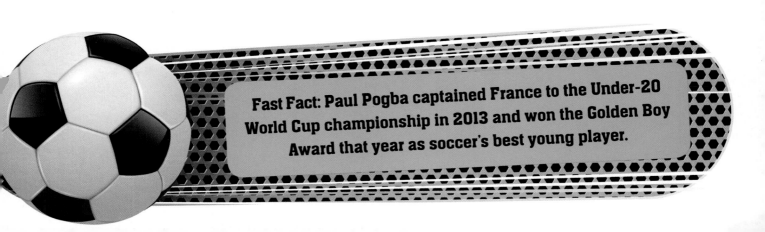

Fast Fact: Paul Pogba captained France to the Under-20 World Cup championship in 2013 and won the Golden Boy Award that year as soccer's best young player.

CHRISTINE SINCLAIR

PORTLAND THORNS FC

Forward
Height: 1.75 m (5'9")
Weight: 68 kg (150 lbs.)
Born: June 12, 1983, in
Burnaby, British Columbia

When captain Christine Sinclair led the Canadian Women's National Team onto the pitch for the bronze medal game at the 2016 Olympics, it marked her 250th international match. Nobody in any team sport has represented Canada on the international stage this many times. Sinclair scored the winning goal in a 2–1 victory over Brazil to give Canada the bronze medal. "I've put everything into this," Sinclair said after the game. "I was not going to leave this tournament without a medal around my neck, [but] I could not have done it without every single member of this team."

Two of Christine Sinclair's uncles played professional soccer, and she started playing when she was only four years old. Sinclair also played basketball and baseball, and she still wears number 12 as a tribute to her favourite player, the Blue Jays Hall of Famer Roberto Alomar.

In 1999, when she was 15 years old, Sinclair attended the Women's World Cup in Portland, Oregon. Two years later she was starting for the women's soccer team at the University of Portland. In four seasons, she set all sorts of scoring records and led Portland to the Women's College Cup championship in 2002 and 2005. As a professional, Sinclair has won championships with the FC Gold Pride (2010), the Western New York Flash (2011) and the Portland Thorns FC (2013).

Sinclair made her first appearance on Canada's National Team in 2000; she was just 16 years old. Since then, she's been a powerhouse as both a forward and midfielder, playing in the Women's World Cup in 2003, 2007, 2011 and 2015. She's also played in the Olympics in 2008, 2012 and 2016. At the 2012 London Olympics, Sinclair was the tournament's top scorer, with six goals. She led Canada to a bronze medal and was selected to carry the country's flag at the closing ceremonies.

Through her strong leadership and dynamic play, Sinclair has raised the profile of her sport in Canada and around the world. With 165 goals and counting, she ranks second in scoring in international women's soccer history.

Fast Fact: In 2012, Christine Sinclair became the first soccer player to win the Lou Marsh Award for Canadian Athlete of the Year.

CONNOR MCDAVID
EDMONTON OILERS

Centre
Height: 1.85 m (6'1")
Weight: 86.5 kg (190 lbs.)
Born: January 13, 1997, in
Richmond Hill, Ontario

Connor McDavid was such a star in minor hockey that in 2012 he became just the third player to be allowed into the Ontario Hockey League Draft as a 15-year-old. McDavid became a star in junior hockey too. In 2014–2015, he helped Canada win the World Junior Championship and was named the Player of the Year in Canadian junior hockey. To no one's surprise, the Edmonton Oilers chose McDavid first overall in the 2015 NHL Entry Draft. After just one season, the Oilers made their 19-year-old star the youngest captain in NHL history when they awarded him the "C" for his sweater on October 5, 2016.

JOHNNY GAUDREAU
CALGARY FLAMES

Left Wing
Height: 1.75 m (5'9")
Weight: 71.5 kg (157 lbs.)
Born: August 13, 1993, in Salem,
New Jersey

Even before the 2011 NHL Entry Draft everyone knew that Johnny Gaudreau was a great player. He had earned the nickname "Johnny Hockey"! Gaudreau is a fast skater who's creative with the puck, but there was one problem: the average size of an NHL forward is 1.85 metres (6 feet,1 inch) and 92 kilograms (202 pounds), and Gaudreau is only 1.75 metres (5 feet, 9 inches) and 71.5 kilograms (157 pounds). His small size scared off enough teams that the Calgary Flames were able to get him in the fourth round of the draft. Gaudreau was named to the NHL All-Rookie Team in 2014–2015 and was a top-10 scorer in 2015–2016, proving that great things can come in small packages.

AARON SANCHEZ
TORONTO BLUE JAYS

Pitcher
Height: 1.93 m (6'4")
Weight: 100 kg (220 lbs.)
Born: July 1, 1992, in
Barstow, California

The Toronto Blue Jays always had high hopes for Aaron Sanchez. When he was only 17, they picked him in the first round of the 2010 MLB Draft. He made his major-league debut in 2014 as a hard-throwing relief pitcher. Sanchez began the 2015 season as a starter, but then found himself back in the bullpen. That winter, a determined Sanchez worked hard to get himself in top physical condition. His efforts paid off in 2016, when he started all year, pitched in the All-Star Game, finished the season with a 15–2 record and led the American League with an ERA of 3.00.

GARY SANCHEZ
NEW YORK YANKEES

Catcher
Height: 1.88 m (6'2")
Weight: 104.5 kg (230 lbs.)
Born: December 2, 1992, in Santo Domingo, Dominican Republic

The New York Yankees boast some of the best sluggers in baseball history, but not even Babe Ruth began with the bang of Gary Sanchez. The Yankees knew early on they had something special in Sanchez. He was just 16 years old when they signed him in 2009 with a $3 million signing bonus. After working his way through their farm system, Sanchez made the majors for good on August 3, 2016. Soon balls were flying out of the ballpark! Sanchez hit 11 home runs in his first 23 games, and he tied an 86-year-old league record when he made it to 20 home runs in just 51 games.

CORY JOSEPH
TORONTO RAPTORS

Guard
Height: 1.90 m (6'3")
Weight: 86.5 kg (190 lbs.)
Born: August 20, 1991, in
Toronto, Ontario

Cory Joseph is just the second Canadian ever to play for the Raptors, and like Jamaal Magloire before him, he was born right in Toronto. Joseph grew up in Pickering, Ontario, and he and his older brother Devoe led Pickering High School to the provincial basketball championships in 2007 and 2008. The next year, Joseph transferred to a school in Nevada to increase his profile in the United States. It worked! Joseph played one year at the University of Texas, and then was drafted into the NBA in 2011. He joined the Toronto Raptors in 2015. Joseph has also represented Canada in several international tournaments and was captain of Team Canada at the 2015 FIBA Americas championship.

KELLY OLYNYK
BOSTON CELTICS

Centre-Forward
Height: 2.13 m (7'0")
Weight: 108 kg (238 lbs.)
Born: April 19, 1991, in
Toronto, Ontario

Standing 2.13 metres (7 feet) tall, Kelly Olynyk grew up in a basketball family. And grew up, and up, and up! His mother refereed women's basketball games and worked for the Toronto Raptors. His father is a long-time coach. When Olynyk was in grade seven, his family moved from Toronto to Kamloops, British Columbia. He became a star at South Kamloops Secondary School and went on to play college basketball in the United States. Olynyk was a First Team All-American at Gonzaga University in 2012–2013, and he was named to the NBA All-Rookie Second Team with the Boston Celtics in 2013–2014. Oylnyk was one of just a few NBA players on the Canadian Men's National Team, which narrowly missed qualifying for the 2016 Olympics.

BRAD SINOPOLI
OTTAWA REDBLACKS

Wide Receiver
Height: 1.93 m (6'4")
Weight: 97.5 kg (215 lbs.)
Born: April 14, 1988, in
Peterborough, Ontario

Brad Sinopoli played AAA hockey for the Peterborough Minor Petes, but ultimately chose football. In 2010, as a quarterback starring at the University of Ottawa, he was named the best university player in Canada. A year later, Sinopoli was drafted by the Calgary Stampeders, and in 2013 they converted him into a wide receiver. He didn't see as much action with the Stampeders as he would have liked, but he did help them win the Grey Cup in 2014. When Sinopoli joined the Ottawa Redblacks in 2015, he became a standout. He caught 86 passes for 1,035 yards and was named the CFL's Most Outstanding Canadian that season, and he did even better in his 2016 season, with 90 receptions for 1,036 yards.

J.J. WATT
HOUSTON TEXANS

Defensive End
Height: 1.95 m (6'5")
Weight: 134 kg (295 lbs.)
Born: March 22, 1989, in
Waukesha, Wisconsin

When Justin James "J.J." Watt played college football, he wanted to score touchdowns. He was a tight end in those days, but his coaches at Central Michigan wanted him to switch to offensive tackle. Watt decided to switch schools instead, and transferred to the University of Wisconsin, where he started playing defensive end. Since being drafted by the Houston Texans in 2011, he's become one of the best defensive players in the NFL. Opposing quarterbacks always have to be wary of Watt, who is the first player in league history to have 20 sacks in two different seasons.

WILL JOHNSON
TORONTO FC

Midfielder
Height: 1.78 m (5'10")
Weight: 72.5 kg (160 lbs.)
Born: January 21, 1987, in
Toronto, Ontario

Will Johnson joined Toronto FC in 2016 and helped his hometown team have its best season ever. Johnson was born in Toronto, but grew up in England and the United States. He began his career in England with the Blackburn Rovers when he was 16. In 2005, Johnson signed with the Chicago Fire in the MLS. He then spent 2006 and 2007 playing in the Netherlands. In 2008, Johnson returned to MLS and had the Goal of the Year while playing for Real Salt Lake. A year later, Johnson played in the All-Star Game and won the MLS Cup with Real Salt Lake. In 2016 he helped Toronto FC reach the post-season for just the second time in the team's ten-year history.

FRASER AIRD
VANCOUVER WHITECAPS FC

Defender / Midfielder
Height: 1.75 m (5'9")
Weight: 70.5 kg (155 lbs.)
Born: February 2, 1995, in
Scarborough, Ontario

Fraser Aird's family has had season tickets for Toronto FC since the team debuted in 2007. Aird was born in Scarborough, Ontario, to soccer-crazy Scottish parents. He moved to Scotland in 2011, when he was 16, to play for the Rangers FC. By the following year, Aird had worked his way up from the Rangers Under-17 team to their men's club. Internationally, he represented Canada at the Under-15 level and Scotland at Under-17 and Under-19 events before joining the Canadian Men's National Team in 2015. In 2016, he was loaned to the Vancouver Whitecaps. Just 21 years old, Aird came on strong during the MLS season.